MARC HELGESEN AND STEVEN BROWN

Active Listening

BUILDING

Skills for Understanding

Student's Book 2

CAMBRIDGE
UNIVERSITY PRESS

To our students, for making the project – and teaching – worthwhile,
To our colleagues, for their many helpful insights, and
To our families, especially Masumi, Kent, Curt, and Clara, for all their support.

PUBLISHED BY THE PRESS SYNDICATE OF THE UNIVERSITY OF CAMBRIDGE
The Pitt Building, Trumpington Street, Cambridge CB2 1RP, United Kingdom

CAMBRIDGE UNIVERSITY PRESS
The Edinburgh Building, Cambridge CB2 2RU, United Kingdom
40 West 20th Street, New York, NY 10011-4211, USA
10 Stamford Road, Oakleigh, Melbourne 3166, Australia

© Cambridge University Press 1994

First published 1994
Fifth printing 1997

Printed in the United States of America

Typeset in Gill Sans and New Baskerville

Library of Congress Cataloging-in-Publication Data
Helgesen, Marc.
Active listening : building skills for understanding (student's
book / Marc Helgesen and Steven Brown.
p.   cm. – (Active listening series)
ISBN 0-521-39882-7
1. Listening – Study and teaching. 2. Listening – Problems,
exercises, etc. 3. Active learning. I. Brown, Steven. II. Title. III. Series.
LB1065.H45 1994
370.15′23 – dc20   93-13274
                                                            CIP

A catalogue record for this book is available from the British Library

ISBN 0 521 39882 7 Student's Book
ISBN 0 521 39885 1 Teacher's Edition
ISBN 0 521 39888 6 Cassettes (available outside North and Central America only)
ISBN 0 521 46680 6 Cassettes (available in North and Central America only)

Book design, layout and design services: Six West Design
Illustrators: Adventure House, Daisy du Puthod, Randy Jones,
        McNally Graphic Design, Wally Neibart, Andrew Toos,
        Sam Viviano

Contents

Plan of Book

	Topics/ Functions	Listening Skills	Grammar/ Vocabulary
Before you begin: How do you learn English?	Explaining types of listening	Listening for gist Listening for specific information Understanding inferences	
Unit 1: Getting to know you	Meeting people	Understanding questions Following instructions Identifying relationships	*Wh*-questions (present) Imperatives
Unit 2: What's your number?	Asking for and giving (numerical) information	Understanding and processing numbers	Numbers
Unit 3: I'm hungry!	Explaining how to make a food	Following instructions Identifying a sequence	Imperatives Sequence markers
Unit 4: Gestures	Describing gestures in different countries	Understanding cultural information Understanding cultural differences	Parts of the body Verbs of motion
Unit 5: Didn't you see that sign?	Stating rules and giving permission	Inferring meaning of signs Understanding rules	Modals: *can* and *should*
Unit 6: How do you feel?	Discussing health and habits	Identifying behavior Understanding suggestions	Simple present Imperatives
Unit 7: Where is it?	Asking for and giving directions	Identifying locations Following directions	Imperatives Prepositions of location
Unit 8: The world market	Discussing exports	Identifying origin Following directions	Adjectives of nationality Prepositions of location Modal: *should*
Unit 9: What do they look like?	Describing how people have changed	Understanding physical descriptions Identifying differences	Descriptive adjectives (people)
Unit 10: What do you do?	Talking about careers and future plans	Identifying occupations Understanding plans Inferring whether a situation is certain	Future with *going to* Future with *will*

	Topics/ Functions	Listening Skills	Grammar/ Vocabulary
Unit 11: **What are they** **talking about?**	Evaluating whether a topic of conversation is appropriate	Inferring topics Understanding relationships	Question forms (simple present)
Unit 12: **How was your** **vacation?**	Describing past activities	Understanding past activities Understanding emotions Following a story	Simple past tense
Unit 13: **Around the house**	Talking about household jobs and chores	Identifying attitudes Identifying preferences	Gerunds (*-ing* forms) Infinitives
Unit 14: **Shopping**	Talking about shopping for clothes and household items	Understanding descriptions Inferring decisions	Existential *to be* Descriptive adjectives (things)
Unit 15: **Going places**	Talking about and comparing countries	Identifying places Understanding questions and answers	Comparatives
Unit 16: **Making plans**	Making and changing plans	Identifying times and places	Future with *will* Future with *going to*
Unit 17: **Youth culture**	Discussing the interests of young people, past and present	Identifying mistakes Understanding details	Past tenses: simple past and past progressive
Unit 18: **Making a** **difference**	Discussing environmental issues	Understanding explanations Understanding details	Simple present Infinitive of purpose (*You use it to. . .*)
Unit 19: **It's in the news.**	Discussing current events	Inferring topics Understanding details	Past tenses: simple past and past progressive
Unit 20: **Dreams and** **screams**	Telling an unusual story	Understanding details Understanding and enjoying a story	Past tenses: simple past and past progressive Sequence markers

Acknowledgments

Culture Corner sources

43   *Book of Lists 3*, by A. Wallace, D. Wallaenchinsky, and I. Wallace. Corgi, 1984.

Illustrations

Adventure House   26, 48/49, 66/67
Daisy de Puthod   4 *(bottom)*, 11, 12, 14, 27/28, 47, 53, 58, 63, 70
Randy Jones   20, 25, 35, 41, 65
McNally Graphic Design   13, 29, 56, 68/69
Wally Neibart   15, 23, 30, 38, 40, 44, 46, 51, 57
Andrew Toos   3, 4 *(top)*, 5, 16, 17, 22, 33, 39, 42, 43, 50, 61
Sam Viviano   8, 32, 34, 36/37, 64

Photographic credits

The authors and publishers are grateful for permission to reproduce the following photographs.

6   *(from left to right)* © H. Gans/The Image Works; © Roy Bishop/Stock Boston; © Larry Dale Gordon/The Image Bank; © Walter Bibikow/The Image Bank
7   *(from left to right)* Rivera Collection/Superstock Inc.; © Hugh Rogers/Monkmeyer Press; © Frank Siteman/Stock Boston
26   Gamma Liaison
31   *(from left to right)* © Nancy Brown/The Image Bank; © P. Cantor/Superstock Inc.
45   © Richard Laird/FPG International
54   *(clockwise from top)* © Butch Martin Inc./The Image Bank; © Michael Melford/The Image Bank; © Gary Crallé/The Image Bank; © Benn Mitchell/The Image Bank; © Janeart Ltd./The Image Bank
59   © 1988 Environmental Defense Fund

Authors' acknowledgments

We would like to thank our **reviewers** for their helpful suggestions: Fred Anderson, Masashi Negishi, Chuck Sandy, and Penny Ur.

We would like to acknowledge the **students** and **teachers** in the following schools and institutes who piloted components of *Active Listening: Building Skills for Understanding*:

Alianza Cultural Uruguay – Estados Unidos, Montevideo, Uruguay; **Central Washington University,** Washington, USA; **Drexel University,** Philadelphia, Pennsylvania, USA; **Fairmont State College,** Fairmont, West Virginia, USA; **Fu Jen University,** Taipei, Taiwan; **Gunma Prefectural Women's University,** Japan; **Impact English,** Santiago, Chile; **Kyoto YMCA (Central Branch),** Kyoto, Japan; **Miyagi Gakuin Women's College,** Sendai, Japan; **Miyagi Gakuin High School,** Sendai, Japan; **National Yunlin Polytechnic Institute,** Yunlin, Taiwan; **Osaka Institute of Technology,** Osaka, Japan; **Queen Alexandra Senior School,** Toronto, Canada; **Santa Clara Educational Options,** Santa Clara, California, USA; **Sendai YMCA English School,** Sendai, Japan; **Suzugamine Women's College,** Hiroshima City, Japan; **Technos International Academy,** Tokyo, Japan; **Tokyo Air Travel School,** Tokyo, Japan; **University of Iowa,** Iowa City, Iowa, USA; **University of Pittsburgh English Language Institute,** Pittsburgh, Pennsylania, USA; **University of South Carolina,** Columbia, South Carolina, USA; **Wen Tzao Ursuline Junior College of Modern Languages,** Taiwan.

Thanks also go to Carmen Begay, Chuck Brochetti, Gerald Couzens, John Day, Marion Delarche, Harumi Fukuda, Brenda Hayashi, Ann Jenkins, Chris Johannes, Kaori Kato, Yuko Kato, Lalitha Manuel, Brian Matisz, Shelly McEvoy, Lionel Menasche, Hiroyuki Miyawaki, Mary Naby, Mark Porter, Sharon Setoguchi, Dorolyn Smith, Noriko Suzuki, Kazue Takahashi, Joseph Tomei, and Paul Wadden.

Finally, special thanks to Suzette André, Mark Chesnut, David Fisher, Deborah Goldblatt, Sandra Graham, Steven Maginn, Susan Ryan, Ellen Shaw, and Mary Vaughn at Cambridge University Press.

To the student

Welcome to *Active Listening: Building Skills for Understanding*. We hope this book will help you learn to listen to English more effectively. You'll practice listening to English. At the same time, you'll learn "how to listen." That is, you'll learn to make use of the English you already know. You'll also think about your reasons for listening. When you do that, listening and understanding become much easier.

This book has twenty units. Each unit has five parts:

- **Warming Up** Warming Up activities will help you remember what you know about the unit topic. This is an important step. It helps you get ready for listening.
- **Listening Task 1** You will listen to people in many different situations. Sometimes you'll listen for specific information such as numbers and places. Other times, you'll have to use what you hear to figure out things that aren't said directly. For example, you'll need to decide how strongly people feel about things they like and dislike.
- **Culture Corner** This is a short reading. It gives information about the unit topic.
- **Listening Task 2** Listening Task 2 is on the same theme as Listening Task 1, but it is a little more challenging.
- **Your Turn to Talk** This is a speaking activity. You will use the language you have just heard. You will do this task in pairs or small groups.

Hints to make you a better listener

- Think about the reason you are listening. Ask yourself, "What do I need to find out?" As you listen, you will do many different tasks. How you listen depends on what you need to find out. Each unit of the book will help you learn to listen. The first unit is called "Before You Begin." It introduces different types of listening. In Units 1–20, every listening task has a box in the top-right corner that tells you the purpose of the activity. The box will help you know what you are listening for.
- The tapes that go with this book are very natural. You won't be able to understand every word. Remember that you don't need to. People don't listen for every word, even in their native languages. The important thing is to think about the meaning of what you hear. You'll understand the most important words. That will help you follow the conversations.
- Many students worry about vocabulary. Of course, vocabulary is important. However, usually you don't need to look up new words in your dictionary the first time you meet them. Here's a good technique: When you hear a word for the first time, ignore it. The second time, try to guess the meaning. If by the third time you listen you still aren't sure, then look it up. This technique will make you more independent.

We hope you enjoy using this book and that you learn how to learn to be a more active, effective listener.

To the teacher

Active Listening: Building Skills for Understanding is a course for low-intermediate to intermediate students of North American English. As the name implies, the course recognizes that listening is a very active process. Learners bring knowledge to class and perform a wide variety of interactive tasks. *Active Listening* can be used as the main text for listening classes or as a supplement in speaking or integrated skills classes.

ABOUT THE BOOK

The book includes twenty units, each with a warm-up activity; two main listening tasks; Culture Corner, a reading passage that presents information related to the unit theme; and Your Turn to Talk, a short speaking activity done in pairs or small groups. In addition, there is an introductory lesson called "Before You Begin." This lesson introduces learning strategies and types of listening, including listening for gist and inference. The lesson is particularly useful for learners whose previous experience has been limited primarily to listening for specific information or to answering literal comprehension questions.

The units can be taught in the order presented or out of sequence to follow the themes of the class or another book it is supplementing. In general, the tasks in the second half of the book are more challenging than those in the first.

Unit Organization

Each unit begins with an activity called **Warming Up**. This activity, usually done in pairs, serves to remind learners of the language they already know. The tasks are designed to activate prior knowledge or "schemata." In the process of doing the warm-up activity, students work from their knowledge and, at the same time, use vocabulary and structures that are connected with a particular function or grammar point. The exercise makes the

listening tasks it precedes easier because the learners are prepared.

Listening Task 1 and **Listening Task 2** are the major listening exercises. The tasks are balanced to include a variety of listening types including listening for gist, identifying specific information, and understanding inferences. The purpose of each task is identified in a box in the top-right corner of each page. Because *Active Listening* features a task-based approach, learners should be doing the activities as they listen, rather than waiting until they have finished listening to a particular segment. To make this easier, writing is kept to a minimum. In most cases, students check boxes, number items, or write only words or short phrases.

Culture Corner is a short reading passage on the theme of the unit. In most cases, you'll want to use it as homework or as a break in classroom routine. Each Culture Corner ends with one or two discussion questions.

Your Turn to Talk, the final section of each unit, is a short, fluency-oriented speaking task done in pairs or small groups. In general, corrections are not appropriate during these activities. However, you may want to note common mistakes and, at the end of the period, write them on the board. Encourage learners to correct themselves.

Hints and techniques

■ Be sure to do the Warming Up section for each unit. This preview can foster a very healthy learning strategy. It teaches students "how to listen." Also, it makes students more successful, which, in turn, motivates and encourages them.

■ In general, you'll only want to play a particular segment one or two times. If the learners are still having difficulty, try telling them the answers. Then play the tape again and let them experience understanding what they heard.

■ If some students find listening very difficult, have them do the task in pairs, helping each other as necessary when possible. The Teacher's Edition contains additional ideas.

■ Some students may not be used to active learning. Those learners may be confused by instructions since they are used to taking a more passive role. Explaining activities is usually the least effective way to give instructions. It is better to demonstrate. For example, give the instruction as briefly as possible (e.g., "Listen. Number the pictures."). Then play the first part of the tape. Stop the tape and elicit the correct answer from the learners. Those who weren't sure what to do will quickly understand. The same technique works for Warming Up and Your Turn to Talk. Lead one pair or group through the first step of the task. The other learners watch. They quickly see what they are supposed to do.

> *Active Listening: Building Skills for Understanding* is accompanied by a *Teacher's Edition* that contains a complete tapescript, step-by-step lesson plans, and expansion activities, as well as grammar and general notes.

HOW STUDENTS LEARN TO LISTEN

Many students find listening to be one of the most difficult skills in English. The following explains some of the ideas incorporated into the book to make students more effective listeners. *Active Listening: Building Skills for Understanding* is designed to help learners make real and rapid progress. Recent research into teaching listening and its related receptive skill, reading, have given insights into how successful students learn foreign/second languages.

Bottom-up vs. top-down processing, a brick-wall analogy

To understand what our students are going through as they learn to listen or read, consider the "bottom-up vs. top-down processing" distinction. The distinction is based on the ways learners process and attempt to understand what they read or hear. With bottom-up processing, students start with the component parts: words, grammar, and the like. Top-down processing is the opposite. Students start from their background knowledge.

This might be better understood by means of a metaphor. Imagine a brick wall. If you are standing at the bottom looking at the wall brick by brick, you can easily see the details. It is difficult, however, to get an overall view of the wall. And, if you come to a missing brick (e.g., an unknown word or unfamiliar structure), you're stuck. If, on the other hand, you're sitting on the top of the wall, you can easily see the landscape. Of course, because of distance, you'll miss some details.

Students, particularly those with years of "classroom English" but little experience in really using the language, try to listen from the bottom up.

They attempt to piece the meaning together, word by word. It is difficult for us, as native and advanced non-native English users, to experience what learners go through. However, try reading the following *from right to left*.

> word one ,slowly English process you When
> to easy is it ,now doing are you as ,time a at
> .word individual each of meaning the catch
> understand to difficult very is it ,However
> .passage the of meaning overall the

You were probably able to understand the paragraph:

> When you process English slowly, one word at a time, as you are doing now, it is easy to catch the meaning of each individual word. However, it is very difficult to understand the overall meaning of the passage.

While reading, however, it is likely that you felt the frustration of bottom-up processing; you had to get each individual part before you could make sense of it. This is similar to what our students experience – and they're having to wrestle with the meaning in a foreign language. Of course, this is an ineffective way to listen since it takes too long. While students are still trying to make sense of what has been said, the speaker keeps going. The students get lost.

Although their processing strategy is a negative, students do come to class with certain strengths. From their years of English study, most have a relatively large, if passive, vocabulary. They also often have a solid receptive knowledge of English grammar. We shouldn't neglect the years of life experience; our learners bring with them a wealth of background knowledge on many topics. These three strengths – vocabulary, grammar, and life experience – can be the tools for effective listening.

The Warming Up activities in *Active Listening* build on those strengths. By engaging the students in active, meaningful prelistening tasks, students integrate bottom-up and top-down processing. They start from meaning, but, in the process of doing the task, they use vocabulary and structures (grammar) connected with the task, topic, or function. The result is an integrated listening strategy.

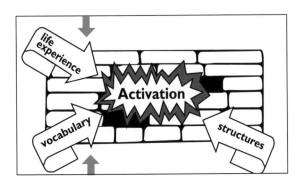

Types of Listening

A second factor that is essential in creating effective listeners is exposing them to a variety of types of listening. Many students have only had experience with listening for literal comprehension. While listening for specific information is an important skill, it represents only one type. We have attempted to reach a balance in the book in order to give students experience with – and an understanding of –

listening for gist and inference. Students usually are quick to understand the idea of listening for gist. They can easily imagine having to catch the general meaning of something they hear. Inference, on the other hand, can be more difficult. Take the following example (from the introductory unit, "Before You Begin"). The students hear the following conversation:

Man:	Let's go outside. We could go for a walk. Maybe we could play tennis.
Woman:	*(with a slight laugh)* Look out the window. It's raining.
Man:	Raining! Oh no!

At a gist level, students can easily identify "the weather" as the main topic of conversation. They are also able to pick out specific information, in this case, the fact that it's raining. To help students understand the idea of inference, ask them whether or not the people will go outside. Students understand that the weather is preventing them from going outside, even though neither the man nor the woman specifically says so.

Many of these ideas are helpful in understanding the listening process, but should not be seen as rigid models. We need to remember that listening is actually very complex. A student listening for gist or inference, for example, may get the clues from catching a couple of specific bits of information.

Of course, learners need practice in listening. But they need more: They need to learn *how* to listen. They need different types of listening strategies and tasks. They need to learn to preview. Our students need exposure to it all. When learners get the exposure they need, they build their listening skills. They become active listeners.

Marc Helgesen
Steven Brown

How do you learn English?

FROM THE PEOPLE WHO WROTE THIS BOOK

Dear students:

We hope that you learn a lot of English. We also hope that you enjoy learning it.

Do you ever think about how you learn? What things do you do to learn English? What techniques help you learn? There are many different ways to try to learn. These are called **strategies**. This book will teach you many different strategies. Think about how you learn best. Try to find the strategies that work best for you.

One strategy is **clarification**. When you ask for clarification, you are "trying to understand." For example, if you don't understand something, you can say, "Could you repeat that?"

Another strategy is **prediction**. Prediction is when you think about what will happen. You guess what you will hear.

In Listening Task 1, you will learn to ask for clarification. But first, try a prediction activity.

Work with a partner.
Look at Listening Task 1 on page 3.
You already know a lot of English.
What do you think the sentences will be?
Say the sentences.

Good luck with learning English. You can do it!

Sincerely,

Marc Helgesen
Steven Brown

LISTENING TASK 1

What do you say when . . . ?

In English, when you don't understand something, you should ask.
There are many ways to ask for clarification.

❑ Look at the questions. What do you think the sentences will be?
Write them.

❑ Now listen. Were you right? Correct the sentences.

What do you say when . . .

Speech bubble on chalkboard: *In listening task 1 you will learn to ask for clarification.*

1. you want someone to say something again?
C<u>ould you</u> <u>repeat</u> that?
E_____ m__ ?
P_____ ?

2. you want to know how to spell a word?
_____ d__ _____ spell (that)?

3. you want to know a word in English?
_____ ____ _____ say (that) in English?

4. you don't understand something?
I don't u_____ .

5. you understand the meaning but don't know
the answer?
__ _____ know.

6. you want the teacher to play the tape again?
Once m_____ p_____ .

CULTURE CORNER

Every culture has different "rules" about asking questions. In some countries, it is
bad to stop the teacher. It means that the teacher didn't explain something very
well. In English-speaking countries (and in English class), it is good – and
important – to stop the teacher or another student. It means you are interested
and are paying attention. In English, it is your job to ask if you don't understand.
In your country, is it OK to ask the teacher questions? How do you feel about
asking questions in English?

3

LISTENING
TASK 2

What are you listening for?

There are many ways to listen. We listen differently for different reasons.

1 Sometimes, you have to understand only the topic or situation.

Example 1 ■ The topic
Listen to the conversation.
What is the most important idea?
Check (✔) your answer.

| ☐ friends | ✔ the weather | ☐ the window |

Example 2 ■ Shopping
Listen. Some people are in a clothing store.
What kind of clothes are they talking about?
Check (✔) your answer.

| ☐ shirts | ☐ sweaters | ☐ ties |

This is called **listening for gist**.
You don't need to understand everything. You just want the
 general meaning.

2 Often, you have to understand specific information.

Example 1 ■ The weather
Listen. What is the weather like? Check (✔) your answer.

☐ It's sunny. ☐ It's snowing. ☐ It's raining.

Example 2 ■ Shopping
Look at the pictures of clothing on page 4.
Listen. How much do the sweaters cost? Write the prices below the pictures.

This is called **listening for specific information**.
Think about what information you need. Ask yourself, "What am I listening for?"

3 Sometimes, the speaker doesn't say the exact words, but you can still understand the meaning.

Example 1 ■ The weather
Listen. Will they go outside? Check (✔) your answer.

☐ Yes   ☐ No

Example 2 ■ Shopping
Look at the pictures of clothing on page 4.
Listen. Which sweater does the woman buy? Circle the one she buys.

This is called **understanding inferences.**
You can understand the meaning even though no one says the exact words.

YOUR TURN TO TALK

Work in pairs. Try speaking only English for two minutes. Choose one of these topics: how I learn English, my free-time activities, or my family. Partner, make sure you understand. Look at page 3 and use as many clarification sentences as you can. Check (✔) the sentences each time you use them. Then change parts.

Example
A: I learn English by watching TV.
B: Could you repeat that?
A: I learn English by watching TV. I always watch American movies . . .

Getting to know you

☐ Work with a partner.
Imagine these people are joining your class.

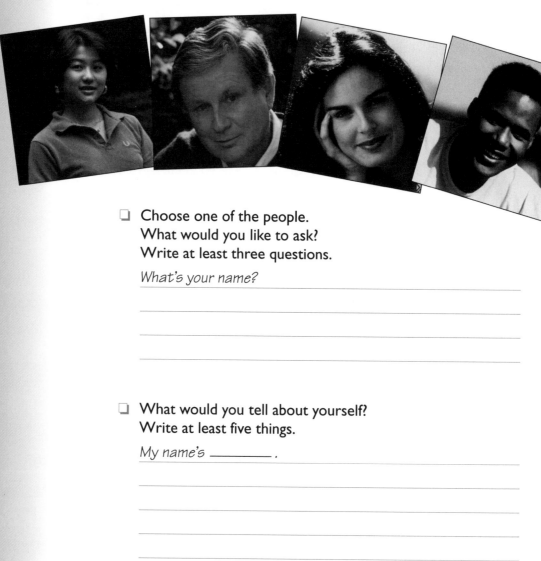

☐ Choose one of the people.
What would you like to ask?
Write at least three questions.

What's your name?

_____

_____

_____

_____

☐ What would you tell about yourself?
Write at least five things.

My name's _____ .

_____

_____

_____

_____

_____

☐ Change partners. Find a classmate you don't know very well.
Ask at least three questions.
Tell your new partner about yourself.

LISTENING TASK 1

How about you?

❏ Listen. Write answers about yourself.

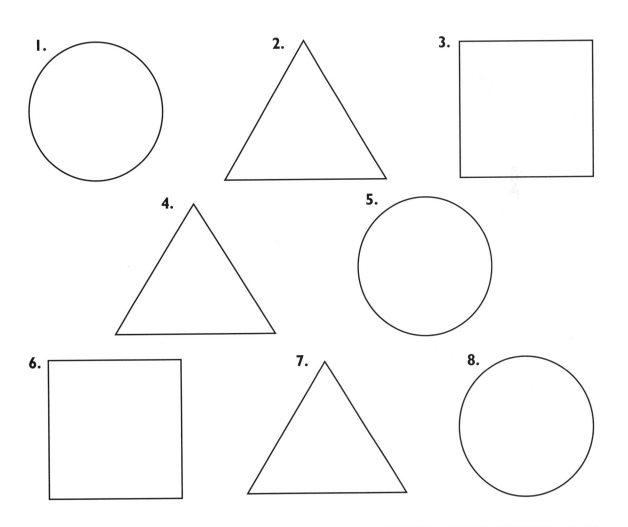

1.

2.

3.

4.

5.

6.

7.

8.

Titles like *Mr.*, *Ms.*, and *Dr.* are usually not used when you say only the person's first name. You might call Tom Johnson *Mr. Johnson* but not *Mr. Tom*. The title *Ms.* is used for both single and married women. Use *Ms.* unless a woman tells you she prefers *Miss* or *Mrs.* What would you call the people in the pictures below?

Amy
Weldon
(your
teacher)

Bill
Jones
(your best
friend)

Jane
Sato
(your
doctor)

LISTENING TASK 2

Friends or strangers?

❑ Listen. Are these people friends or strangers?
Write "F" for "friends" and "S" for "strangers."

1. ___F___

2. _____

3. _____

4. _____

5. _____

6. _____

YOUR TURN TO TALK

Work with a partner. Look at your partner's answers to Listening Task 1, "How about you?" on page 7. Which answers are interesting? Ask questions about the answers. Try to learn at least five new things about your partner.

Sample questions

What does this mean?

Why do you want to go there?

Where did you meet _____ *(name)* ?

How often do you . . . ?

What's your number?

❏ Write these numbers.

Your telephone number: _____

Your address: _____

_____

JUNE

Name _Mia_____

Date _21st_____

Occasion _18th birthday_

Gift Idea _blouse – size 32_

Name _Kent_____

Date _23rd_____

Occasion _21st birthday_

Gift Idea _soccer ball_

Name _Mom and Dad_

Date _16th_____

Occasion _25th anniversary_

Gift Idea _silver pin?_

JUNE

Name _Tom_____

Date _2nd_____

Occasion _graduation_

Gift Idea _English dictionary_

Name _____

日 本 国
JAPAN

国 際 自 動 車 交 通
INTERNATIONAL MOTOR TRAFFIC

国 際 運 転 免 許 証
INTERNATIONAL DRIVING PERMIT

1949年9月19日の道路交通に関する条約
CONVENTION ON ROAD TRAFFIC OF 19 SEPTEMBER 1949

MIYAGI, JAPAN

Issued at ____ FEB. 19, 1992   228208095330
Date of Issue
92   345

宮 城 県 公 安
MIYAGI PREFECTURAL PUB

AMS2281898

UN 1 ONE
DOLLAR
CANADA

Faucett
THE FIRST AIRLINE OF PERU

F. Morales
NAME   NOMBRE   NOM

804 North Alta Vista Street
ADDRESS   DOMICILIO   DOMICILE

Los Angeles, CA 90046   USA
CITY VILLE CIUDAD   COUNTRY PAYS PAIS

BANCO
DE
ESPAÑA

MIL
pesetas   1000

Membership No. _17864_
Exp. _1-17-94_

THE WORLD
OF VIDEO

Tele. (212) 691-1581

❏ What other numbers are important to you?
   Dates? Times? Ages? Prices? Height? What else?
Write some of them. Don't write what they mean.
Don't write any "secret" numbers like bank accounts.

_____   _____   _____

_____   _____   _____

_____   _____   _____

❏ Work with a partner.
Read your numbers.
Partner, write the numbers you hear.
Then say what you think they mean.

May I ask your number?

❏ Listen. Find the correct form for each conversation.
Write the missing numbers in the correct places.

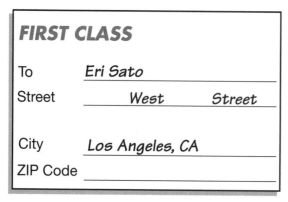

FIRST CLASS

To   *Eri Sato*

Street   *West*   *Street*

City   *Los Angeles, CA*

ZIP Code _____

a. a mailing label

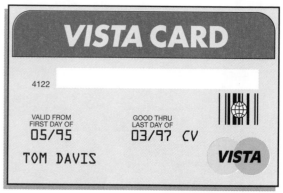

VISTA CARD

4122

| VALID FROM FIRST DAY OF | GOOD THRU LAST DAY OF |
| 05/95 | 03/97 CV |

TOM DAVIS

VISTA

b. a credit card

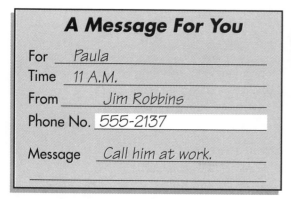

A Message For You

For   *Paula*
Time   *11 A.M.*
From   *Jim Robbins*
Phone No.   *555-2137*

Message   *Call him at work.*

c. a telephone message pad

Clark University
Student Identification Card

Lisa Marks
Student ID number

          -

Lisa Marks
Student Signature

Valid:
Spring
Semester

d. a student ID card

LISTENING TASK 2

Fast math

❑ Listen. Write the numbers.
How fast can you figure out the answers?
Try to write the answers before you hear them.

1.   389
   + __56__
     445

2. _____
   + _____
   _____

3. _____
   + _____
   _____

4. _____
   × _____
   _____

5. _____
   × _____
   _____

6. _____
   × _____
   _____

❑ Now listen to two conversations in a department store.
Figure out the totals before you hear them.
Write the prices.

7. $ ___.___
   × _____
   $ ___.___

8. $ ___.___
   + ___.___
   $ ___.___

YOUR TURN TO TALK

Work in groups of four. Each person in the group says a number larger than 100. Write the numbers. Then add them. Who can add the fastest? Did you all get the same total? Continue with new numbers.

Example
A: 125
B: 242
C: 560
D: 329
B: I got 1257.
C: No, that's not right. It's 1256.

I'm hungry!

WARMING UP

What is your favorite food?
How do you make it?

❑ Work with a partner.
   Tell your partner how to make the food.
   Use some of these words:

bake   boil   peel

cut   slice   chop

fry   stir   put in

Food: _____

First, _____

Then, _____

Next, _____

After that, _____

Finally, _____

LISTENING TASK 1

Now that's a sandwich!

❑ Listen. What ingredients go in this sandwich?
Write or draw them.

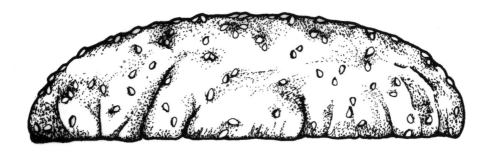

Roast beef

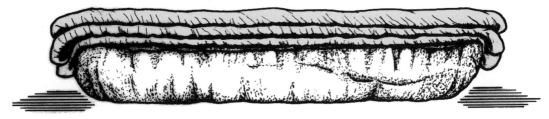

When people in the United States and Canada talk about "sandwiches," they think of two pieces of bread with something in the middle – cheese, meat, or vegetables. However, cultures around the world use bread – or something like it – to make delicious meals you can hold in your hand. In Mexico, people eat tacos, flat tortillas wrapped around meat and vegetables. People in southern Asia (India, Pakistan) fill many kinds of breads with spicy curries. In the Middle East, people eat pita or pocket bread full of vegetables. Are sandwiches popular in your country? What kind?

What's cooking?

Shrimp Jambalaya

Ingredients:
1 piece of beef (chopped)
2 tablespoons butter
1 large onion
1/4 cup celery
1 green pepper
2 large tomatoes
2 cloves garlic
2 cups chicken broth
2 cups shrimp
2 cups of rice (uncooked)

Spices:
chili powder
white pepper
black pepper
cayenne pepper
Tabasco sauce
salt

❏ Listen. Some students are learning how to make jambalaya, a dish from the southern part of the United States.
Put the pictures in order (1–9).

YOUR TURN TO TALK

On another piece of paper, write one food for each:

1. a kind of sandwich
2. a fruit you like
3. a dessert
4. a vegetable you like
5. a kind of salad
6. a drink
7. seafood
8. a food you don't like
9. a kind of meat

Now, work in groups of three. Find out what foods your classmates wrote. How many people wrote the same thing?

Sample questions

What kind of sandwich did you write?   What did you write for number 2?

Gestures

WARMING UP

❑ Work with a partner.
Look at these gestures from the United States and Canada.
Are there gestures for these meanings in your country?
Do the gestures.

Gestures are actions you do with your hands or head.
They have different meanings in different cultures.

Goodbye.
Yes.
Money!
I'm surprised.
Come here.

❑ What other gestures do you use?
Write the meanings.

_____

_____

_____

_____

15

1. In most countries . . .
a *nod* means

☑ yes.
☐ no.   *Greece*

2. In Tonga . . .
raised eyebrows mean

☐ yes.
☐ money.

3. In Argentina . . .
tapping your head means

☐ that person's crazy!
☐ I'm thinking.

4. In the Netherlands . . .
tapping your elbow means

☐ that person doesn't want to
spend money.

☐ you can't depend on that person.

LISTENING TASK 1

What does that mean?

One person in each conversation above uses a gesture.
The first speaker is on the left.

☐ Listen. What do the gestures mean in these places?
Check (✔) the correct meaning (1–8).

CULTURE CORNER

Sometimes the same gesture can have very different meanings in different cultures. For example, in the United States and Canada, it is common to make a circle with your thumb and first finger. It means "OK." In Japan, the same sign means "money." In southern France, it stands for "zero" or "worthless." Be careful! If you travel to Brazil or Greece, do not use this sign. It has a very bad meaning. Are there gestures that you should not use in your country?

5. In most parts of Europe . . .
circling your head means

- ☐ that person's crazy.
- ☐ there's a telephone call.

6. In Italy ...
flicking your chin means

- ☐ I don't know.
- ☐ go away!

7. In the United States . . .
thumbs up means

- ☐ something bad.
- ☐ everything is OK.

8. In Germany . . .
tossing your head means

- ☐ no.
- ☐ yes.
- ☐ come here.

LISTENING TASK **2**

It's different there.

☐ Listen. In some places, the gestures have a different meaning.
Write the names of the countries next to the meanings (1–8).
Use these countries:

Brazil	Canada	Colombia	Greece
India	Italy	the Netherlands	Nigeria
Peru	Spain	Taiwan	

YOUR TURN TO **TALK**

Work in groups of three. How many gestures can you think of? Write at least 15.
Then think of a story. Your story should include at least eight of the gestures.
Practice pantomiming the story. Then pantomime it to another group. They will
try to guess the story.

Didn't you see that sign?

WARMING UP

Signs should be easy to understand.
These aren't.

❏ Work with a partner.
Look at the signs.
What do you think they mean?

1.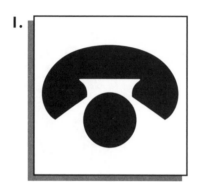

2.

3.

4.

❏ Check your answers at the bottom of page 20.

18

What do they really mean?

❑ What do you think these signs mean?
Check (✔) the correct box.

❑ Now listen. What *do* the signs mean?
Circle the answers.

1.
   ☐ Recreation/exercise area
   ☐ Do not enter.

2.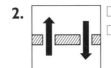
   ☐ Elevator
   ☐ Stay on the left.

3.
   ☐ You can turn your car around.
   ☐ Point of interest

4.
   ☐ Lock your car.
   ☐ Rent a car

5.
   ☐ Earthquake area
   ☐ Unusual nature site

6.
   ☐ Old building
   ☐ Chemicals

7.
   ☐ The water is deep.
   ☐ No swimming.

8.
   ☐ Meeting place
   ☐ Crossroad

You can't do that.

Rangers work in parks and campgrounds.
They take care of the park and make sure people are safe.

❏ Listen. A ranger is explaining the park rules.
Some things in the picture are against the rules.
Cross out (**X**) the activities that are against the rules.

YOUR TURN TO TALK

There are many kinds of rules: laws (the speed limit when driving, where you can and can't smoke), school rules ("You must come to class," "You have to do homework"), personal rules ("I always do my homework before I watch TV"), rules of right and wrong ("Don't lie"). Work in groups of five. What laws and school rules do you have to follow? What are your personal rules and rules of right and wrong? Write as many rules as you can in five minutes. Have you broken any of these rules? Which ones? Why?

Meanings of signs on page 18: **1.** There is a public telephone. **2.** You must keep to the right. **3.** Customs. You must have your baggage checked. **4.** Up escalator.

How do you feel?

❑ Work with a partner.
Ask the questions in the survey.
Check (✔) the answers for your partner.

✝ Health Notes

How Healthy Are You?

	Yes	No
1. Do you smoke?	❑	❑
2. Do you have a checkup at your doctor's office once a year?	❑	❑
3. Do you sleep more than 10 hours a day?	❑	❑
4. Do you sleep less than 5 hours a day?	❑	❑
5. Do you exercise (cycling, walking, swimming, dancing, etc.) more than 20 minutes at least three times a week?	❑	❑
6. Do you live in a city?	❑	❑
7. Do you work more than 10 hours a day?	❑	❑
8. Is your life stressful?	❑	❑

❑ Add up your partner's score.
Add one point for each "yes" answer to
questions 2 and 5.
Add one point for each "no" answer to
questions 1, 3, 4, 6, 7, and 8.

Partner's score _____
6–8 points = You're probably healthy.
3–5 points = You could do better.
0–2 points = Be careful!

LISTENING TASK 1

I really should be more careful.

❏ Listen. Two friends are talking about health.
Do they do these things? Write "yes" or "no."

	June	Andy
1. smoke	no	yes
2. visit the doctor	____	____
 **3.** sleep too much	____	____
 **4.** sleep too little	____	____
5. exercise	____	____
6. live in a city	____	____
7. work too much	____	____
8. have a lot of stress	____	____

CULTURE CORNER

Exercise is an important part of staying healthy. In the United States and Canada, the most popular ways to exercise include walking (22% of Americans and Canadians walk for exercise), swimming (17%), bicycling (13%), running/jogging (11%), and playing tennis (9%). Staying healthy isn't the only reason people exercise. Other reasons are:

to feel better	80%	to reduce stress	62%
to look better	48%	to have more confidence	33%

Do you exercise? What kinds of exercise are popular in your country?

LISTENING TASK 2
Stressed out

❏ Listen. Mia is feeling a lot of stress.
Which things does her friend suggest? Check (✔) them.
What does she say about each idea? Write one thing.

✔ exercise
ride a bicycle

☐ see a doctor

☐ learn yoga

☐ change your job

☐ have more fun

☐ take vitamins

YOUR TURN TO TALK

Work in groups of four. What do people in your group do to stay healthy? How many different things have people done in the past week? List them. In your class, which group can list the most items? What are the most popular ways to stay healthy?

Where is it?

❏ Work with a partner.
Think of places in your town or area.
Don't say the names of the places.
Give directions to the places.
Start at a well-known building.

Partner, follow the directions. Guess the places.
What are the places? Write them.

_____

_____

_____

Go past the bank.

Turn right at the hospital.

Go straight three blocks.

It's on the southwest corner.

Turn left at the second traffic light.

YOU ARE HERE

Drawing by Chas. Addams; © 1974
The New Yorker Magazine, Inc.

LISTENING TASK 1

The park

☐ Listen. Where are these places? Write the numbers on the map.

1. the playground

2. the boat rental

3. a telephone booth

4. the hot dog stand

5. the beach

6. the zoo entrance

CITY PARK

YOU ARE HERE

CULTURE CORNER

NORWAY 14MI
DENMARK 23MI
SWEDEN 25MI

Where in the world would you see this? You're 14 miles (23 km) from Norway. Sweden is only 25 miles (40 km) away, and Denmark is even closer – 23 miles (37 km). You might think the sign is in Northern Europe. But it also says you're 37 miles (60 km) from Mexico, 46 miles (74 km) from Peru, and only 94 miles (151 km) from China. Actually, this unusual sign is in Maine in the United States. The places on the sign aren't the countries and famous cities. They're names of towns in the area! Are there places with unusual names in your country?

How do I get there?

The Hotel Lotte is in Seoul, Korea.
It is a large and busy hotel.

❏ Listen. Some guests are at the front desk.
They are asking for directions to these 5 places.
Follow the directions. Write the numbers on the map.

1. The Bank of Korea
2. The Jung-an Map Shop
3. The British Embassy
4. The National Museum
5. The Chongmyo Shrines

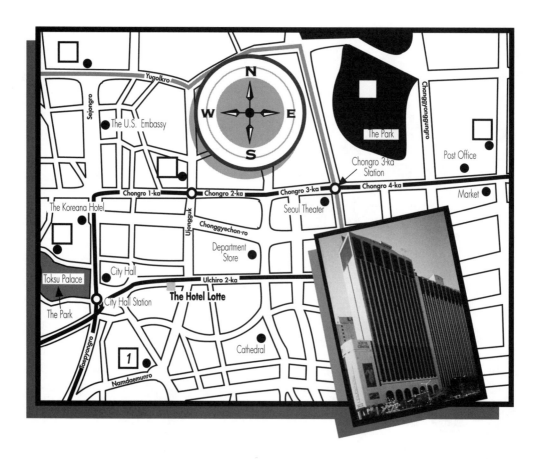

Work with a partner. What are the five most interesting places for a visitor to your town or area? First list them. Explain why they're interesting. Then join another group. Combine your lists. Choose the three most interesting places. Think of directions for tourists. Start at the building you're in or another well-known place.

Example

A: How do you get to _____ ?

B: Well, walk out of the door and turn _____ . . .

The world market

WARMING UP

Exports are products that countries sell to other countries.
Sometimes exports are surprising.

❏ Work in groups of three.
Can you guess the biggest exports of the countries?
One person is game leader. Leader, look at page 70.
The others use this page. Play the game.

EXPORT CHALLENGE

Look at the products. Each product is the biggest export of one of these countries:

Australia	the Bahamas	Canada	China
France	India	Italy	Mexico
Norway	the Philippines	Spain	Thailand

Take turns. Guess the country which sells more of each product than any other product. (Cross out the country after a correct guess. There are two extra countries listed.)

PRODUCTS:

1. rice

2. beef

3. wheat

4. oil

5. cotton

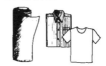
6. clothing and cloth

7. fruit

8. diamonds

9. lobster

10. electronic equipment

Each correct answer = 1 point.
Your points: _____

World Trade Expo!

People are shopping at an international trade fair. Each country has a display.

❏ Listen. What countries are selling these products? Write the nationalities.

Brazilian	Canadian	French	German	Italian
Japanese	Korean	Spanish	Taiwanese	U.S.

1. leather shoes and bags
Spanish

2. cameras

3. lumber and wood products

4. computers

5. watches

6. TVs and video players

7. chemicals

8. coffee

CULTURE CORNER

International trade is important to nearly every country in the world. Sometimes it is difficult to really know where a product comes from. For example, 28 percent of Japanese cars sold in the United States are actually built in U.S. factories, not in Japan. Ten percent of cars from Chrysler – a large U.S. car company – are made in other countries. When companies send products to other countries, they need to think about many things, like prices, local styles, and taxes. Perhaps the most important thing to think about is quality. When people buy something expensive and like it, they usually tell eight other people. When they don't like it, they tell 22 others! What products does your country sell around the world?

Where can I find that?

❑ Listen. The shoppers in Listening Task 1 are asking directions.
Write the countries in the correct places.

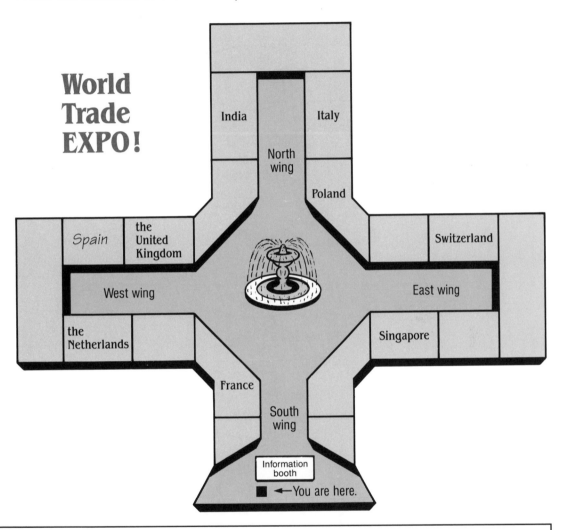

World Trade EXPO!

India Italy

North wing

Poland

Spain the United Kingdom

Switzerland

West wing East wing

the Netherlands

Singapore

France

South wing

Information booth

■ ←You are here.

YOUR TURN TO TALK

Work in groups of three. You have seven minutes. How many countries and nationalities can you think of? What languages are spoken in the countries? Which group could think of the most countries, nationalities, and languages?

Examples

Country	*Nationality*	*Language(s)*
Canada	Canadian	English, French
Brazil	Brazilian	Portuguese
Japan	Japanese	Japanese

29

What do they look like?

❏ Work in groups of three.
What words do you use to describe people?
Write at least two more words for each group below.

1.
- wavy
- straight
- **hair**
- black

2.
- tall
- heavy set
- **body type**

3.
- brown eyes
- glasses
- **face**

LISTENING TASK 1

They've changed a little.

❑ Listen. Two friends are talking about these people.
The people have changed since these pictures were taken.
Circle what has changed.

CULTURE CORNER

The way we describe people is sometimes based on culture. For example, in Thailand, when you tell a middle-aged man, "You look a little fat," it has a good meaning. It means, "You must be doing well and have a lot of food." In the United States and Canada, the meaning is bad: "You are eating too much and not taking care of yourself." What kind of descriptions have good meanings in your culture? Bad meanings?

That's different!

❑ These pictures are not the same.
Look at the pictures for 30 seconds.
How many differences can you find? Circle them.

❑ Now listen. Circle the other differences.

YOUR TURN TO TALK

Work with a partner. Look at your partner for exactly one minute. Try to remember everything about your partner's clothing and appearance. Then sit back-to-back so you can't see each other. Ask questions. See how much your partner remembers.

Sample questions
Do you remember what color my shirt is?
Do my shoes have laces?

What do you do?

 WARMING UP

❑ Look at the jobs.
Pick two that are similar in some way.
Draw a line between these jobs.

Example
a chef ——————— *an artist*
The reason: They're both creative.

❑ Pick four more pairs that are similar.
Draw lines between them.

a computer
programmer

a department
store clerk

a lawyer

a secretary

a bank teller

a chef

—————————————————

an artist

a police officer

a politician

a businessperson

a doctor

❑ Work with a partner.
Look at your partner's pairs.
Guess the way each pair is the same.

33

LISTENING TASK 1

Who are they talking to?

❏ Listen. Who are these people talking to?
Write the occupations on the line.
What words helped you know?
Write one or two words under each line.

1. _a waiter or waitress_

    fish   vegetable   rice

2. _____

3. _____

4. _____

5. _____

6. _____

CULTURE CORNER

The titles of some jobs are changing. The old names made the jobs sound as if they were only for men or only for women. The new names are the same for both males and females.

Old	*New*
airline stewardess/steward	flight attendant
fireman	fire fighter
mailman	letter carrier/post office clerk
policeman/woman	police officer
salesman/woman	sales clerk/sales representative

Have any jobs changed names in your country? What was the reason?

LISTENING TASK 2

I'm going to become a programmer.

❑ Listen. These students are talking about jobs after graduation.
What are they going to become? How sure are they?
Check "yes," "maybe," or "no" for each profession.

| Maria | Kent | Diane | Tony |

	Yes	Maybe	No
1. Maria			
a computer programmer	✔	❑	❑
2. Kent			
a teacher	❑	❑	❑
an artist	❑	❑	❑
3. Diane			
a lawyer	❑	❑	❑
a politician	❑	❑	❑
4. Tony			
a chef	❑	❑	❑
a restaurant owner	❑	❑	❑

YOUR TURN TO TALK

Work in groups of five. Think of a job. Partners, ask yes-no questions about the job.
When an answer is "yes," try to guess the job. Take turns choosing different jobs.

Example

Q: Is the job dangerous?   A: No.
Q: Do you make a lot of money?   A: Yes.
Q: Are you a lawyer?   A: Yes.

35

What are they talking about?

❑ Work with a partner.

What do you usually talk about when you meet someone for the first time?

What don't you talk about?

Check (✔) "yes" or "no" for each topic below and on page 37.

> This is a great party, isn't it?

the place you are at

☐ yes   ☐ no

> What do you do?

jobs

☐ yes   ☐ no

> How much money do you make?

salary

☐ yes   ☐ no

> Would you like something to drink?

food and drink

☐ yes   ☐ no

> Do you believe in God?

religion

☐ yes   ☐ no

> Where are you from?

hometowns

☐ yes   ☐ no

LISTENING TASK 1

I wouldn't ask that.

❏ Listen. What are these people talking about?
Circle the topics.

❏ Look at the topics you circled.
Did you check "yes" for these topics in Warming Up?
Look at the topics you didn't circle.
In English-speaking countries, people don't usually talk about these topics
when they first meet.

> Beautiful weather
> we're having.

weather
☐ yes   ☐ no

> How old are you?

age
☐ yes   ☐ no

> Are you married?

lifestyles
☐ yes   ☐ no

> Do you like jazz?

likes and dislikes
☐ yes   ☐ no

> Are you going to
> have children?

personal decisions
☐ yes   ☐ no

In English-speaking countries, it is usually OK to introduce yourself to other
people in class or at a party. You don't need to wait for someone to introduce
you. When people meet for the first time, they sometimes talk about the
situation before they introduce themselves. For example, they may find
something they agree on:

A: I think this will be an interesting class.
B: I think so too. By the way, I'm Jean.

How do you meet new people in your country? Do you introduce yourself?

LISTENING TASK 2

A day in the life . . .

❏ Listen. Meg and Ted have a lot of different conversations during the day.
Who is Meg or Ted talking to? Match each conversation (1–6) with a picture.
Write the number in the box. There is one extra picture.
What helped you understand? Write at least one thing for each.

coffee

wife talking about plans for
the day

Work in groups of three. How many ways do you know to introduce yourself in
English? What else do you say when you meet someone for the first time?
Write your answers. Which are formal? Which are friendly?

Examples
I'm very pleased to meet you. (*formal*)
Hi. (*friendly*)

How was your vacation?

❑ What did you do on your last vacation?
Check (✔) the things you did.
Add something about each activity.

✔
- ☐ went hiking
- ☐ visited a museum
- ☐ visited relatives
- ☐ saw a movie
- ☐ went to a beach
- ☐ just rested
- ☐ went shopping
- ☐ read a book
- ☐ went camping
- ☐ visited a garden
- ☐ visited a famous place
- ☐ other

❑ Work with a partner.
What activities did your partner check?
Ask your partner about the vacation.
Write three things your partner did.

_____

_____

_____

LISTENING TASK 1

Did you have a good time?

❑ Listen. People are talking about their vacations.
Draw lines to the things they did.
Did they enjoy themselves? Complete the sentences.

I.

Kenji's vacation was
great

Laura's vacation was
_____

2.

Lisa's vacation was
_____

Dave's vacation was
_____

Holidays are special days like New Year's when most people don't work. They
include cultural, religious, and historical days. Vacation days are days that a
person takes off from work. Work hours, holidays, and vacations differ a lot
around the world. This chart shows averages for five countries.

Country	Work week	Holidays	Vacation
Britain and France	39 hours	8 days	25 days
Germany	38	10	30
Japan	42	20	16
The United States	40	10	12

How many hours a week do people work in your country? How much vacation
do they have?

LISTENING TASK 2

A weekend to remember (unfortunately)

❏ Listen. Tom went camping last weekend.
He didn't have a good time.
Put the pictures in order (1–8).

YOUR TURN TO TALK

Work in groups of five. You are going to tell a chain story. It should be an adventure story. One person begins. That person says the first sentence. Start like this:

Once upon a time ___(name)___ went to ___(place)___.

Someone else says the next sentence. Each person adds a new sentence to the story. Use some of these words:

skiing	crocodile	helicopter	president or prime minister
ice cream	beautiful	bomb	flamingo
expensive	birthday	gold	

41

Around the house

What jobs do you enjoy doing at home?
Which do you dislike doing?

❑ Look at these household tasks.
Which do you dislike? Cross (**X**) them out.
Are there any you like? Circle them.

	cleaning		cooking
	doing laundry		vacuuming
	washing dishes		washing windows

❑ Write at least three more household tasks.
Do you like to do them or not?

_____

_____

_____

❑ Work with a partner.
How many of your answers were the same?
Which tasks do you like the most?
Which do you hate?

LISTENING TASK 1

I hate doing that!

❏ Listen. People are talking about jobs around the house and other chores.
Do they like them or dislike them?
Draw lines to show how strongly they feel.

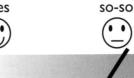

likes   so-so   dislikes

1. cooking

2. washing floors

3. giving the baby a bath

4. doing laundry

5. washing dishes

6. cleaning the office

These are the 10 most unpopular household tasks in the United States and
Canada. The percentage shows the number of people who dislike this task more
than any other.

1. washing dishes	17.0%	6. vacuuming	6.2%
2. cleaning the bathroom	8.8	7. washing windows	4.9
3. ironing	8.5	8. cooking	4.8
4. washing floors	7.5	9. doing laundry	4.7
5. cleaning	7.3	10. dusting	4.7

What jobs around the house do you think are the most unpopular in your country?

CULTURE CORNER

43

LISTENING TASK 2 *I agree!*

❏ Listen. Does the man like these things?
Check (✔) "likes" or "dislikes."
Why? Write his reasons.

❏ Do you agree? Circle "I agree" or "I don't agree."

Your opinion

1. Working at home
- ✔ likes
- ❏ dislikes

Why? *quieter, doesn't have to drive*

I agree.
I don't agree.

2. Cooking
- ❏ likes
- ❏ dislikes

Why?_____

I agree.
I don't agree.

3. Reading nonfiction
- ❏ likes
- ❏ dislikes

Why?_____

I agree.
I don't agree.

4. Growing flowers
- ❏ likes
- ❏ dislikes

Why?_____

I agree.
I don't agree.

5. Driving
- ❏ likes
- ❏ dislikes

Why?_____

I agree.
I don't agree.

YOUR TURN TO TALK

Imagine your "dream house." What would it have? A swimming pool? A marble fireplace? A big yard? A tennis court? Think for one minute. Then work in groups of three. Describe your dream houses. What features do you all want? What do your partners want that you don't?

Shopping

WARMING UP

This is a shopping survey.
It asks about your shopping habits.

❏ Work with a partner.
First write your answers.
Then ask your partner the questions.
Write your partner's answers.

Shopping Survey

	You	Your partner
1. Do you enjoy shopping?	_____	_____
2. How often do you go shopping?	_____ (times a week/month)	_____
3. What do you like to shop for?	_____	_____
4. Do you like to shop alone or with someone?	_____	_____
5. Have you ever shopped by mail or telephone?	_____	_____

LISTENING TASK 1

It's perfect!

❏ Listen. Some people are shopping. What are they buying?
Match each conversation (1–5) with a picture.
Write the number in the box. There are three extra pictures.

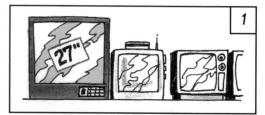 **1**

CULTURE CORNER

Most cultures have sayings about money. In the English-speaking world, people say "A penny saved is a penny earned." A penny is one cent. It isn't worth very much, but the proverb says even small amounts are valuable. The Japanese have a similar saying: "If you laugh at one yen, you will cry for one yen." A saying from Britain warns about being too worried about spending money. It is "Penny wise but pound foolish." It means that if you always buy the cheapest thing or try not to spend a penny, you will end up spending a pound – 100 times as much. Money is important in most cultures. How important? In India there is this saying: "If you say 'money,' even the dead will come alive." Are there sayings about money in your language?

LISTENING TASK 2 *I'll take it.*

❑ Listen. People are shopping.
Do you think they will buy these things?
Circle "yes" or "no." When the answer is "no," write the reason.

1. the jacket

yes   (no)

He doesn't like the design.

2. the CD player

yes   no

3. the cordless phone

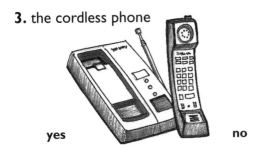

yes   no

4. the jeans

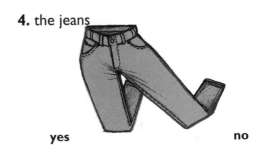

yes   no

5. the computer

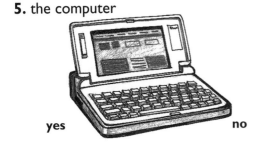

yes   no

6. the notebook

yes   no

YOUR TURN TO TALK

Work in groups of three. Imagine that you are buying gifts. Think of one gift for each category below. What would you buy? Where would you buy it? Who would you give it to?

something expensive   something very cheap
something funny or crazy   something practical and useful
something romantic   something for your teacher

Going places

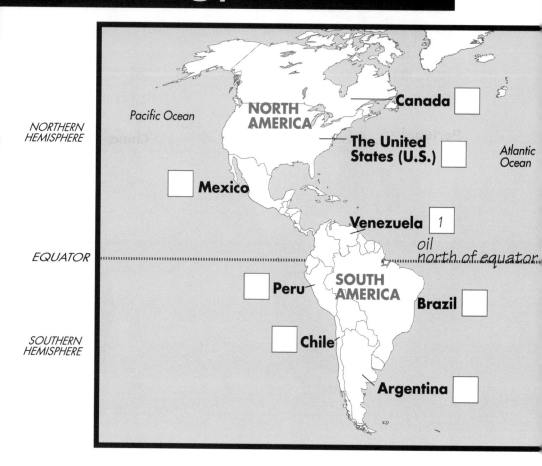

NORTHERN
HEMISPHERE

Pacific Ocean

NORTH AMERICA

Canada

The United States (U.S.)

Atlantic Ocean

Mexico

Venezuela 1

oil
north of equator

EQUATOR

Peru

SOUTH AMERICA

Brazil

Chile

SOUTHERN
HEMISPHERE

Argentina

WARMING UP

❑ Work with a partner.
Answer these questions. Listen to your partner's answers.
(Other countries are labeled on pages 66 and 67.)

1. If you could go to any country in the world, where would you go?
2. What country would you not want to visit? Why?
3. Which place in your country is the most interesting for tourists from other countries?
4. What things about your country are hard for foreigners to understand?

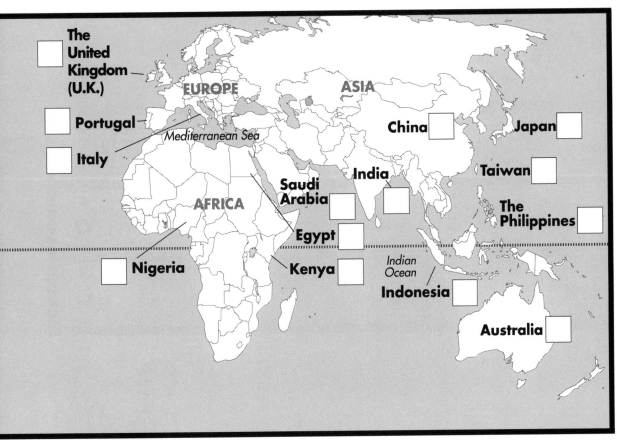

The
United
Kingdom
(U.K.) ☐

EUROPE

ASIA

Portugal ☐

China ☐

Japan ☐

Italy ☐

Mediterranean Sea

India

Taiwan ☐

Saudi
Arabia ☐

AFRICA

The
Philippines ☐

Egypt ☐

Nigeria ☐

Kenya ☐

Indian
Ocean

Indonesia ☐

Australia ☐

LISTENING TASK 1

How much do you know?

❑ Listen. You are going to take a "quiz" on countries.
Look at the map. Which countries is the speaker talking about?
Write the numbers in the boxes.
What information helped you guess each country? Write your answers.

CULTURE CORNER

In the year 1578, Beijing was the world's largest city. It had 707,000 people. In the 1800s, London was the largest. It grew from 1,117,290 in 1801 to a peak of 8,615,050 in 1939. In 1957, Tokyo had the most people: 8,415,400. Now the world's four largest urban areas are Tokyo (27 million), São Paulo (18 million), Seoul (16 million), and Mexico City (15 million). What is your country's largest city? Why have people come to live there?

49

LISTENING TASK 2

Game show

❑ Listen. Two people are playing a TV game show.
What are the correct answers? Write each country or place.
Who gets the points? Check **X** for the woman's points.
Check **O** for the man's points.

1 ☐**X** ☐**O**	2 ☐**X** ☐**O**	3 ☐**X** ☐**O**
4 ☐**X** ☐**O**	*Thailand* 5 ☑**X** ☐**O**	6 ☐**X** ☐**O**
7 ☐**X** ☐**O**	8 ☐**X** ☐**O**	9 ☐**X** ☐**O**

YOUR TURN TO TALK

Work with a partner. This is a speaking contest. See how long you can speak.
Your turn is over when you say something that is not in English or you stop for five seconds. Choose a topic:
• The place I would most like to visit.
• The best place for tourists in my country.
Your partner will listen and keep time. Then your partner speaks. When you finish, find a new partner and begin again.

Making plans

❑ Will you do any of these things this month?
Check (✔) the ones you'll do.
When? Write your answers.

❑ Work with a partner.
Which things will your partner do? When?

	You	When	Your partner	When
Go to a party				
Take a trip				
Do something you don't want to do				
See a movie or video				
Watch or play sports				
Go to a restaurant with a friend				
Do something that will make you tired				
Go to a concert				

❑ Which of your partner's answers were the most interesting?
Ask at least two more questions about them.

Can we change the time?

❑ Listen. Some people have a change in plans.
Cross out the old information.
Write the new information.

1.

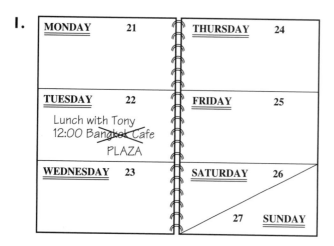

MONDAY	21	THURSDAY	24
TUESDAY	22	FRIDAY	25

TUESDAY 22
Lunch with Tony
~~12:00 Bangkok Cafe~~
PLAZA

WEDNESDAY 23

FRIDAY 25

SATURDAY 26

27 SUNDAY

2.

THURSDAY _____

FRIDAY _____
Concert 7:30 Hayes Hall
Meet in front

SATURDAY _____

3.

Departures			
Flight	Destination	Time	Gate
UA528	Tokyo	4:16	6
NA475	Seattle	4:25	12
NW723	Toronto	4:40	7
CN305	São Paulo	4:50	5
CA39	Taipei	5:10	11

4.

SUN	MON	TUE	WED	THU	FRI	SAT
			1	2	3	4
5	6	7	8	9	10	11
12	13	14	15	16	17	18
				23	24	25

20
2:30
Dr. Lee

21

Customs about time differ greatly around the world. In the United States and Canada, you should be on time for a business meeting, but a little (10 or 15 minutes) late if you are invited to a party at someone's house. Never arrive at a party early. But when meeting friends somewhere, in a restaurant for example, try to arrive on time. What are some of the time customs in your country?

CULTURE CORNER

LISTENING TASK 2 — Monday morning!

❏ Listen. A secretary is taking telephone messages.
Write the changes on the schedule.

Monday, April 12

Time		Time	
9:30		2:00	↓
10:00	Ms. Riviera	2:30	Ms. Perry
10:30	~~Mr. Long~~	3:00	Meeting with Dr. Chung
11:00	Mr. Black	3:30	
11:30	**Mr. Long**	4:00	Mr. Michaels
12:00	Mr. Rogers	4:30	Ms. Sato
12:30	Mr. Franks	5:00	HOSPITAL
1:00	LUNCH	5:30	
1:30	↓	6:00	↓

YOUR TURN TO TALK

As a full class, think of at least 10 places or events you could invite a friend to.
Then stand up and find a partner. Invite your partner to one of the places or events.
Partner, flip a coin and give your answer:

 = Say yes.
Decide the time.

 = Say no.
Give an excuse.

Change partners. Continue until you have invited 10 different people. How many
times did people accept your invitations?

Example

    A: Would you like to go to _____ on Saturday?
 (Y) B: That sounds good. What time?
(or)(N)   Sorry, I'd really like to, but I have to work.

Youth culture

❏ Work with a partner.
Think about young people in your country.
What is popular with them?
How many things can you list for each topic?

music _rock, especially musicians like..._

clothing _____

food _____

free-time activities _____

places _____

sports _____

LISTENING TASK 1

Jeans

❏ Read this story.
Now listen.
There are 10 mistakes. The tape is correct.
Find the mistakes. Write the correct information.

Jeans: The "Uniform" of Youth

Jeans are very popular with young people all over the ~~United States~~. *world* Some people say that jeans are the "uniform" of youth. But they haven't always been blue.

The story of jeans started almost 200 years ago. People in Genoa, Italy, made pants. The cloth made in Genoa was called "jeanos." The pants were called "jeans." In 1850, a salesman in California began selling pants made of canvas. His name was Levi Strauss. Because they were so strong, "Levi's pants" became popular with gold miners, farmers, and students. Six years later, Levi began making his pants with a blue cotton cloth called denim. Soon after, factory workers in the United States and Asia began wearing jeans. Young people usually didn't wear them.

In the 1950s, two people helped make jeans popular with teenagers: Elvis Presley, the king of rock and roll, and James Dean, a famous TV star. Elvis wore tight jeans.

Most parents didn't like Elvis or his jeans. But teenagers loved him and started to dress like him. In *Rebel Without a Cause*, James Dean wore jeans. He was a hero to many young people.

During the 1960s, rock and roll became even more popular. Young people had more money. Their clothes showed their independence. Some people decorated their jeans with colorful patches and designs.

In the '70s and '80s, jeans became very expensive. In addition to the regular brands like Levi's and Lee, famous designers like Calvin Klein and Pierre Cardin began making "designer jeans." They were very stylish and very fashionable.

Jeans are so popular that Levi's has sold over 10 billion pairs. Almost anywhere in the world you know what young people want to wear: jeans!

CULTURE CORNER

Young people in most countries are interested in entertainment. In the United States and Canada, people under 25 spend about 6 percent of their income on entertainment. Of that money, about one-third is used for tickets for movies, concerts, and other events. A little more than one-third is used for things like stereos, video players, and televisions. Reading is also popular. Young people spend nearly 10 percent of their entertainment income on books and magazines. What do young people in your country like to spend money on?

Rock and roll!

❑ Look at the covers of the CDs.
Do you know anything about these types of popular music?

❑ Listen. A music expert is talking about the history of popular music.
When did each type of music become popular? Write the dates on the lines.
Write one or more facts about each type.

mid-1950s

popular on radio

19

19

19

19

19

19

19

YOUR TURN TO TALK

Think about young people in your country. Do they often disagree with their parents? What kinds of things do parents and young people disagree about? Write five ideas. Then work in groups of five. Combine lists. Which ideas are the same? Which are different?

Making a difference

WARMING UP

❏ Work with a partner.
What can people do to help save energy and stop pollution?
How many things can you think of?
Write them.

⚡	**To save electricity?** *Turn off the lights when they are not in use.*
🌲	**To save trees?** *Recycle paper.*
⛽	**To save gasoline?**
🗑	**To make less garbage?**

❏ Which things do you usually do?
Circle them.

Little things help.

❑ Look at the pictures. What could you do with these things to help the earth?

❑ Now listen. People are talking about improving the environment.
What do they do with these things? Fill in the blanks.

1. newspapers

Recycle them.

2. cups

_____ Styrofoam cups.

3. bags

Use cloth bags instead of
_____ or _____ bags.

4. plastic bottles

Use in the _____
tank to save water.

5. an air pressure gauge

Check _____ ; it saves
_____ .

CULTURE CORNER

These are things people in the United States do to help the environment.

	Regularly	Sometimes	Never
Recycle cans and bottles	64%	19%	17%
Buy environmentally safe products	53	31	15
Recycle newspapers	50	14	36
Buy recycled products	47	30	22
Give money to environmental groups	18	30	51
Carpool (share rides) to work/school	17	12	70

What kinds of things do you do in your country?

 **Recycling**

❑ Listen to this radio announcement.
How much of these materials do people in the United States use?
Fill in the blanks.

Newspapers

Office and writing paper

Glass bottles

Plastic bottles

Aluminum

Leaves and grass

Iron and steel

aluminum: enough to rebuild all _commercial airplanes_ every three months

iron and steel: enough to supply all of our _____ makers

newspapers: _____ trees a week

office and writing paper: enough to build a wall from _____ to _____

leaves and grass: _____ tons each year

glass: enough to fill _____ buildings in New York City every two weeks

plastic: _____ plastic bottles every hour

What things do you do to help the environment? What do other people do? What do you wish more people would do? What other issues are you interested in? Social issues? Local issues? Work with a partner. Discuss your ideas for one minute. Then change partners. Discuss your ideas with your new partner.

It's in the news.

WARMING UP

❏ Work with a partner.
Think about recent news stories.
What is the most important news story for each topic?
Write your answers.
Write extra facts about one news story.

	News Story	Extra Facts
International news		
National news		
Local news		
Sports		
Music, art, or science		

LEADERS OPEN TALKS IN QUEBEC

Mayor backs new plan

Scientists find new cure

STUDENTS STAGE PROTEST

Soccer finals to be played in Spain

UN HELPS AID EFFORTS

What are they talking about?

❑ Listen. People are talking about newspaper articles.
What is the order of the stories?
Number the pictures (1– 4). Write extra facts about each story.
There are two extra pictures.

1

rock musician running
for mayor

Headlines in English language newspapers can be difficult to understand. Headlines usually are not in complete sentences. Short words like "a," an," "the," and the verb "to be" aren't usually used. Sometimes special words are used to save space. These are some common ones (with their meanings):

head (leader)
hit (criticize or affect badly)
key (important)

push or back (support or encourage)
talks (negotiations)

Examples
Agency head pushes peace talks = The leader of an agency encourages peace negotiations.
Key trade plan hit = An important trade plan is criticized.

What is difficult to understand in newspapers in your language?

LISTENING TASK 2

The six o'clock news

❏ Read these newspaper stories.
Then listen to the news on the radio.
Write the missing information.
The type of information you need is in [blue].

1.

COUNTRIES ARGUE OVER FARM PRODUCT IMPORTS

[City] _Paris_ – The leaders of the seven major industrialized nations met today to discuss trade problems. The key issue is imported agricultural products. Nearly half of the countries attending the Paris conference are protesting pressure to open their markets to foreign farm products, especially [type] _____ . Little progress is expected to be made in this area. Several leaders are facing elections this year and farm voters are demanding protection.

2.

Rock star runs for mayor

[City] _____ – Rock star Jerry Ward announced today that he is entering the mayor's race. Ward hopes to use his popularity as well as his public support of striking [type] _____ workers to make up for his late start in the elections. Ward says he knows what the people want because rock is the music of the people. His campaign slogan is "From the concert hall to City Hall, Jerry's with you."

3.

Bulldogs down Wildcats

Vancouver – The Vancouver Bulldogs beat the Portland Wildcats [game score]____ to ____ Tuesday night.

The winning pitcher was Juan Sanchez. It was his second win of the season. Bryce pitched for the Wildcats. The Bulldogs are the only team that hasn't lost this season. They will play the San José [team] _____ tomorrow.

4.

Airline pilot locked out

[City] _____ – Passengers on Transglobal Airlines flight [number] _____ , while waiting for take-off at the airport, were surprised by a loud banging on the plane's door. When the crew checked, they found the plane's pilot, who had been locked out.

YOUR TURN TO TALK

Work in groups of three. You are radio news announcers. Think of a recent news story that most people know about. First practice telling the story. Then change groups. Tell your story to your new group. Partners, listen. Option: Change three or more facts in the news story. Partners, try to find the changes.

Dreams and screams

❏ Are you afraid of these things?
Check (✔) your answers.

	Yes	A little	Not at all
spiders	☐	☐	☐
high places	☐	☐	☐
snakes	☐	☐	☐
big dogs	☐	☐	☐
storms/thunder	☐	☐	☐
dark, lonely roads	☐	☐	☐
airplanes	☐	☐	☐
the ocean	☐	☐	☐
going to the dentist	☐	☐	☐

❏ Work in a group of 6–10 people.
Compare answers.
Which things are the scariest to your group?

LISTENING **TASK** 1

That's strange.

❑ Listen to two stories about unusual creatures.
Write three or more facts about each story.

1. Space creatures

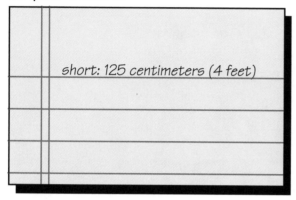

short: 125 centimeters (4 feet)

2. The Loch Ness monster

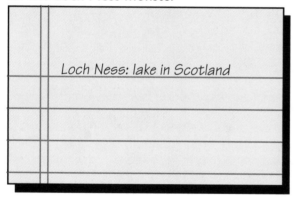

Loch Ness: lake in Scotland

©SAM VIVIANO 1993

❑ Do you think UFOs and space creatures are real?   Yes ☐   No ☐

Do you believe in the Loch Ness monster?   Yes ☐   No ☐

CULTURE CORNER

Many cultures have "monsters." Asian and European cultures have stories about dragons. In both cultures, dragons guard the doors to places full of riches (money and gold). Pictures of dragons are often painted on doors and gates. In Europe, the dragons never give their money away. In Asia, dragons often give presents. The Western dragon is evil, but the Eastern dragon can be kind and is a symbol of luck. In European cultures, dragons usually live alone. In Asian cultures, they live together in societies. What monsters do you tell stories about in your country?

Wait until the master comes.

❏ Look at the words and pictures.
What do you think the story is about?

❏ Listen to the story.

old man
the woods
got lost
old house
rain
made a fire
sleep
a cat
another cat
"Shall we do it now?"
"Wait until the master comes."
a larger cat
the fourth cat
in front of the door
"It's almost time."
window
runs
"At last, I'm safe!"

Ramsey Jones 93...

❏ Did you like this story?   Yes ☐   No ☐

Was it scary?   Yes ☐   No ☐

YOUR TURN TO TALK

Work in groups of four. Did you like "Wait Until the Master Comes"? Was it scary? Everyone, give an opinion. Tell why or why not. Then each person tells a story. It can be one you know or one you make up.

World map

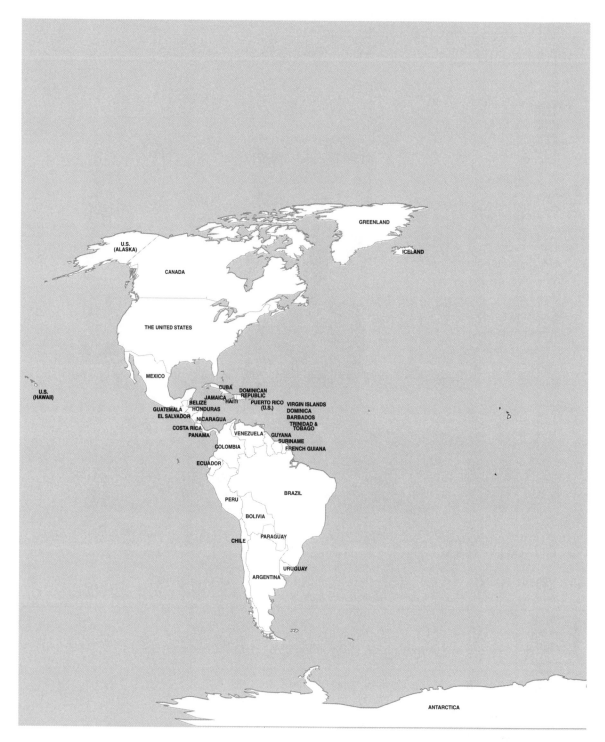

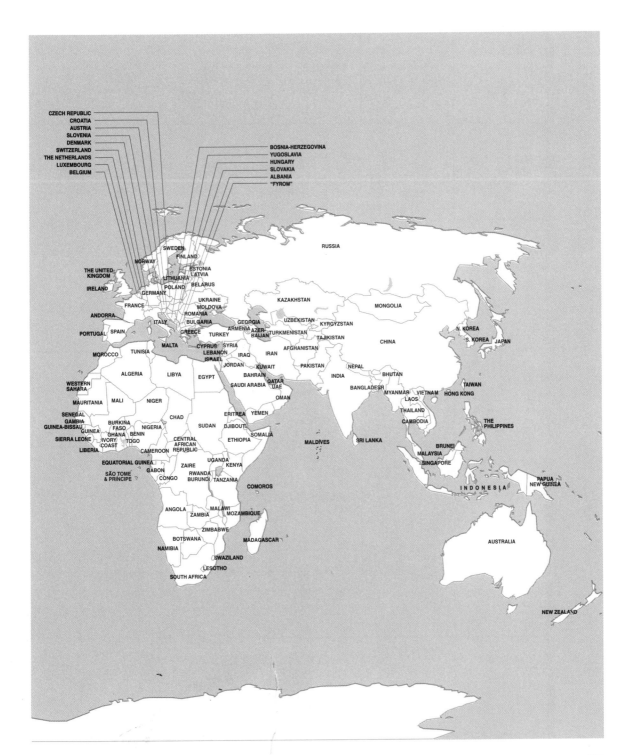

Activation:
a speaking and listening game

Start here ➡	What are you going to do next weekend?	Tell about your best friend.	What free-time activities do you like?	What 3 foods are most typical of your country?

The *Activation* game

- Work in groups of 3 or 4.
- Each player needs a place marker.
- Put the marker on "Start here."
- Close your eyes. Touch the "How many spaces?" box with a pencil. Move that many spaces.
- Read the sentence(s). Answer with at least 3 things.
- Each partner asks one question about what you said.
- When you land on a TEAMWORK space, everyone answers.
- If someone else lands on the same TEAMWORK space, any player can ask that person a question.
- Take turns.

What is the most important recent news story?

Tell about a vacation you'd like to take. ✈

What is a rule that many people don't follow?

Who do you respect?

Do you want to change anything about the way you look? What is it?

TEAMWORK
Each person says a number larger than 1,000. Then everyone tries to add all the numbers. Who is the fastest?
- Do this 3 times.

What do you do that makes the world better?

What don't you like shopping for?

What job around the house do you hate to do? ☹

???????????
Any player can ask you one question.
???????????

Have you ever been very sick? When? What did you do?

???????????
You can ask one question to any player.
???????????

Do you know a scary story? What is it about?

Tell about an English lesson where you learned a lot.

TEAMWORK
What do you do (or should you do) to help the environment?

| Give directions to your favorite restaurant. | Tell about a food you liked when you were a child. | What is your favorite kind of music? ♪ 𝄞 ♫ | What do you enjoy shopping for? | **TEAMWORK** How many gestures can you think of in 1 minute? Say what they mean. |

| What is the most difficult part of learning English? | | | | Tell about something you didn't need but bought anyway. |

| | | *How many spaces?* | | Tell about a time you felt really good. |

			2 1 3 1 3 2	
			1 3 4 2 3 1	What do your parents look like?
			3 1 2 1 2 3	
			1 2 1 3 5 2	
			3 5 2 1 2 3	
			2 1 3 4 3 1	

How many spaces?

2	1	3	1	3	2
1	3	4	2	3	1
3	1	2	1	2	3
1	2	1	3	5	2
3	5	2	1	2	3
2	1	3	4	3	1

| What rule or law don't you like? | What is (or was) your favorite subject in school? | What is the most exciting job in the world? | ???????????? You can ask one question to any player. ???????????? | **TEAMWORK** How many things do you have with you that are from other countries? |

| Tell about something that happened while you were traveling. | What do you do on Sundays? | Can you tell a story or joke in English? | Do you know a gesture from another country? What is it? | **TEAMWORK** What do you do for your health? List as many things as you can in 1 minute. |

| What do you like about another culture? | Give directions to a place you like. | ???????????? Any player can ask you one question. ???????????? | What job around the house should you do today? Will you? | What is your favorite way to get the news? |

The world market: game leader

WARMING UP

❏ You are the game leader.
Ask the questions and keep score.
Your partners will guess the answers. (They use page 27.)

Example
Leader: What country's biggest export is rice?
Student 1: China.
Leader: No, that's not right.
Student 2: Thailand.
Leader: That's right. You get one point.

EXPORT CHALLENGE

Look at the products. Each product is the biggest export of one of these countries:

Australia	the Bahamas	Canada	China
France	India	Italy	Mexico
Norway	the Philippines	Spain	Thailand

Take turns. Guess the country which sells more of each product than any other product. (Cross out the country after a correct guess. There are two extra countries listed.)

PRODUCTS:

1. rice   *Thailand*

2. beef   *Australia*

3. wheat   *Canada*

4. oil   *Norway*

5. cotton   *Mexico*

6. clothing and cloth
France

7. fruit   *Spain*

8. diamonds   *India*

9. lobster   *the Bahamas*

10. electronic equipment
the Philippines

Each correct answer = 1 point.
Your points: _____